MW00815054

WRITERS REPUBLIC

PERMISSION TO

Heal

CHANTELI ORTIZ

WRITERS REPUBLIC L.L.C.
515 Summit Ave. Unit R1
Union City, NJ 07087, USA

Website: *www.writersrepublic.com*
Hotline: *1-877-656-6838*
Email: *info@writersrepublic.com*

Ordering Information:
Quantity sales. Special discounts are available on quantity purchases by corporations, associations, and others. For details, contact the publisher at the address above.

Library of Congress Control Number: IN-PROCESS
ISBN-13:   978-1-63728-345-5   [Paperback Edition]
                  978-1-63728-346-2   [Digital Edition]

Rev. date: 03/18/2021

to those who lay awake at night wondering why they weren't enough.

I want to thank each person who encouraged me to share my work time and time again.

To my significant other, who has always been the one to love and support me. To my friend and mentor, Clare, who has always pushed me to express myself and find my outlet.

To my family and friends who always stuck by my side even in my darkest moments.

To my Vavo who left this earth way too soon, I know you're smiling down at me from heaven. I only wish you could be here with me today.

Most importantly, to those who read this book and relate to it in any way, shape or form.

Remember your worth. Remember love is always on the way.

you're broken
i cut my tongue on your lips
you're made of glass
you're so venomous
toxic to my heart
savior to my soul
your hands, my love
why are they always cold?
your eyes, dead and mean
parts of you, unseen
they say you're no good for me
that i should give you up
please don't destroy me
and say that it's your love

i promised i would wait for you
but you don't love me back
do you think of me too?
tell me, what did i lack?

love is a losing game
and i guess we played it strange
your heart was filled with needles
and shards of glass
i knew we wouldn't last
but there was still hope

put your mistakes in the past
use forgiveness as your soap
love is bittersweet
and it hurts so much
i miss how our lips met
and how i felt from your touch
that rainy october day
in your arms, it was bliss

i silently begged you would stay
all your flaws, i dismissed
your mind is a maze
and i got lost a few times
we will live on, always
forever, through this passage

you broke my heart into a million pieces.
so why do i still smile at the thought of you?

 i should hate you.

i stare at the city through encased glass
holding my breath as i remember the past
his hands pressed against this window as he wept
i begged him to stay as he slept
his breath quick and sharp
as his fist penetrated the wall
his life was never simple
he told me it all
he painted pictures
but only in grey
he said he hated color
cause all it'd do was fade
i told him i'd wait
until he becomes who he's supposed to be
but he said i was stupid
that he will never be able to love me
his past took a toll on him
and i hate it so much
because i'd die for him
but he doesn't believe in love

we were passing ships on a foggy night
both equally as damaged as the other
i had parts that could fix you
this you knew

the first collision terrified me
and i know it scared you too
we talk of dreams under a starry sky
i tell you of things i usually hide
you were my saving grace
and that's where i went wrong

i'd like to believe i knew who you were
that every girl after me wouldn't dare to dive so deep

you kept on moving and call it quits
i waited for you and got nothing
but a broken heart and a sunken ship

the curl of my hair blocks my vision
he stands a few feet away, lost in thought
i love storms... but he fears thunder
all this time against me, he fought

the water is cold against my skin
i know he fears not loving me
as he keeps eyes upon the sea
his heart is cold as he admits his sin

my heart beats rapidly against my rib cage
all of my nightmares become true
those five words my pride won't allow me to say
come back, i miss you.

when love isn't enough

i remembered that you were broken. and i remember that i said i would always be there. i remember the way your hands felt in my hair and i remember the way your breath sounded in my ear. i remembered what it felt like to love you. you weren't easy and i never wanted easy. you were complicated and suppressed. you threw away my heart of gold, i had to keep repeating to myself that night, "my love, you have a heart. my love, i know this hurts. but one day it won't anymore."

i remembered the sound of your laughter at 4am when my hair was doing that static thing it always does. i remember the distance between us when you told me your heart felt heavy. i remember pleading in my head, "stay. i love you. we can get through it. oh my god please stay." i remember that i didn't say any of those things. i remembered that i loved you more than anyone else did, isn't that enough? and i remember the way my heart cracked when you said it wasn't.

love him gently
keep him safe
love him deeply
find his place

fight for emotion
in his eyes
fight for the happy
he tends to hide

let him know
you're there forever
not like the last girl
who mimicked the weather
tell him he's a storm
thunder in human form
tell him he's going to make it
mend his heart, don't break it

don't fall in love with a writer

don't fall in love with a writer, they'll write you love letters and poems in the back of their math notebook. they'll wake up at 4am everyday just to make sure you get that good morning text. they'll read romance novels and think of the color of your eyes when people mention heaven. they'll see you in their morning cup of coffee. your bed becomes their favorite place. their journal pages all are about you and the way your nose curves. the way you speak, the way your heart breaks when you think of your father. and when you leave?

oh, their bedroom floor is littered with unfinished poems, dotted with tears from the ghost of love. they'll wake up in the middle of the night and call for you. their chest will get heavy every time someone mentions your name. and remember those romance novels? they can't read those anymore. it hurts too much to remember.
so please. please don't fall in love with a writer if you know you won't stay.

the moon sings to me as i lose myself in book pages. my mind
is drawn to you. old lovers, they holler names: the names that
broke their heart in two. and i'm among them, shouting yours.
i wish upon a dozen fallen stars. i wish to love you again. i
wish to hear your chuckle like i had once before. it seems like
a lifetime ago when we were in love. or when i was in love and
you were just passing time.
i stand among the fools; who pity others like them. for only a
fool can understand foolishness. people like us, we have glass
hearts and steel souls. we have tiredness embedded into our
being, stressing out over missed opportunities.
in the midst of you breaking my heart, i glorified your
bluntness. i remember that was why i fell for you in the first
place.
you, with your electric soul and vice of hearts. i wince at your
name. i never knew it was possible to be in love with someone
you absolutely despise.
i love you, even though i shouldn't.

i don't want you to be happy

i don't want you to be just "happy". i don't want you to feel a temporal joy. i want you to carry the world in your hands. i want you to feel like the first breath of fresh air. i want you to be the morning cup of coffee. i want you to be the first sentence of a new book. i want you to be the photographs of lovers. i want you to be the passion of an artist.

i want your heart to be golden and your eyes to see every inch of the universe. i want the stars to align your name. i want the oceans to calm at your touch. i want you to be the prayer for every problem. i want you to be yellow roses amongst the red. i want you to never fear the world. i want the world to love you entirely for everything you are.

so no, i do not want you to be just "happy".

i want you to be the fucking sun.

when i look at you, i can't tell if i despise you.
or if i'm madly in love with you.

i never learned the difference.

unexpected happenings

when i awoke this morning i didn't expect to miss you. i didn't
expect to feel the loss of us so deep in my chest. when i awoke
this morning i didn't expect to be here, right now, in this
shallow motel pool singing the love songs we used to listen to.
i didn't expect to write this. i didn't expect to drink seven cups
of coffee and i didn't expect that i'd tear up at the sight of your
face. when i awoke this morning i didn't expect to be swerving
down the highway blasting *that* rap song, the one my best
friend and i sang at the top of our lungs, both sad over boys
who broke our hearts. the song that most reminded me of you.
i didn't expect to be singing all the words to christian music
with my mother outside a convenience store at nine o'clock at
night.
i didn't expect to stop caring. i didn't expect to allow myself to
get hurt, over and over. so i stopped allowing it.
and it hurts every day you don't come back.
so i don't expect it anymore.

hope

you'll love many other people
and maybe they'll hurt you too
but there will be someone who makes all the hurt worth it.

i'm bound to you

i'm bound to you and there's nothing worse than that. with everything i do, i keep you in mind. the day after we broke up and my best friend begged me to go to this party with her. i didn't feel like going but my heart hurt and i wanted to forget it all. that night an old friend kissed me in the middle of an overcrowded dance floor. i ran outside hyperventilating, tears rushing down my face.
i called you three times.
you didn't pick up.
i just kept repeating at the ringing: "i'm sorry. oh my god. i'm so sorry. i love you. i'm sorry."
i guess it's a good thing you didn't pick up, how stupid would i have sounded? i'm almost positive your voicemail caught me screaming "fuck you" in a fit of rage. i wanted so badly to run to you. i wanted to hear your voice, my world was crashing down and all i could think about was the way you pronounced my name. i wanted to tell you that i loved you. my friends say i should move on. i can't even stomach the thought. when you're in love no one else matters. i guess you know that as well as anyone huh?
i'm bound to you.
and it hurts more than anything because you're bound to someone else.

12:21 am
here i am once again
conjuring up pretty words
in an attempt to keep our love alive.
i refuse to let go

everytime i close my eyes
i get visions of you
in my room, near my books
skimming all of them for highlighted words
you always did say i had a beautiful mind.

there are days where i feel like i'm over it
and then there are days where i stare at my wall
remembering how it felt to love you dearly
my fingernails are painted your favorite color
i didn't do that on purpose
there are days i feel like i'm over it
but then i put on your shirt and cry
i don't think i'm over it

loving you didn't feel like love

i tried to justify why i loved you so dearly. i remembered the day you told me everything that happened to you. i was at this music festival, surrounded by boys who wanted to be with me and here i was, texting you, waiting for you. my heart sunk once you were finished with your story. "i'm sorry," i said. "i wish i could've changed that for you." i wanted to cradle you in my arms and sing you the lullabies you never heard as a child. that night i texted my best friend. "i want him to have one good thing." she replied immediately. "perhaps you could be that good thing."

i froze.

how could i be good for you? how could i mend you when i was still picking up all the pieces of myself? how could i possibly affect you? i decided to take the chance. i decided to love you. i don't regret it. being with you felt like all the emotions at once; it felt like sadness, anger, joy ... it felt like being alive. loving you? felt like the room i ran to when my parents were fighting. loving you felt like a storm that i just wanted to get lost in. loving you didn't feel like love. it felt like chaos.

broken sea shells

they say the best way to mend a broken heart is to distract yourself. create new goals. find a purpose. whatever you do, don't distract yourself with another person because when they inevitably leave it'll hurt worse than the first time.

i distracted myself by cleaning. i cleaned every inch of my house that day. my mother thought it was great. how can I tell her it was so the thoughts wouldn't swallow me whole?

i distracted myself by partying. i went to seventeen parties when you left. i lost the thoughts of your eyes in the crowd of hormonal teenagers. the music drowns out the sound of your voice. "i love you. i don't want to live in a world without you." the music drowns out the lies you told.

i distracted myself by riding the carousel on a december afternoon with the girl who's heart hurt as much as mines did. we laughed so hard that day.

i made my escape to the beach and picked up every pretty seashell. but i never once kept a broken one. and i guess that what went wrong with us.

i was broken and you never wanted to keep me.

when i say, i want the best for you.
it doesn't mean i wasn't the best for you
i was everything i could have been for you
i gave you everything i had
so maybe i might not have been the one for you
and that's okay
i'll find myself and my soulmate one day
but keep in mind, i tried to give you the world
and that is a lot coming from a broken girl

sometimes when my heart breaks
for the millionth time over
i need to remind myself
of the words i've written long ago

i need to remind myself
that each day without him
is a day i learn to be independent
and a day closer to being happy with myself

i guess this is letting go.

the healing.

today
i woke up
and i realized i deserve better

there will be days
where your heart feels heavy
and your eyes have bags under them
there will be days
where you hate him
and you want revenge
there will be days
nothing makes sense
and there will be days
where this won't hurt anymore

this is called healing.

thank you to the boys who broke my heart
my mind a book, my pain turned into art
all those nights i spent crying in bed
i regret letting him get into my head
i do not need love if it means pain
and i will not allow myself to play this game

i know this hurts, i know you are broken
but you begin to heal once pain is spoken
this is a lesson for me, to the next boy
this is the last time i will be treated like a toy
i am beautiful, i am worth much more
than a boy who makes my eyes pour

you loved me
and left me
all in the same breath

i deserve more than that

being with you
was the calm before the storm
being with you
was pure uncertainty
being with you
felt like waiting for rain during a drought
being with you
was absolutely stressful
and i've come to realize
being with you
wasn't what love should've been
so i no longer want to be with you.

to move on
is to accept
that life isn't always fair
and to move on
is to accept
that the universe has a person for you
beautifully crafted and amazing
to move on
is to give up your hope
in order to get reassurance

darling, move on

there will come a day
where you show up at my door
and ask me to stay
to try again, once more
my heart will beat in my chest
i put on a facade
but i want to say yes
our love was too flawed
i'll watch your eyes
as they glaze over
i'll remember the lies
and the pain of october
you hurt me and you didn't care
i was so broken
damaged beyond repair
i demand that you leave
but you won't budge
you get on your knees
and beg for us to love
"i'm no longer that girl"
tears spill down your face
"i am a dazzling pearl
and beautiful black lace"
i shut the door
and you disappear
i fall to the floor
and sigh in despair

this is strength

i'm sorry
that every time you say "i love you"
i tell you that you're sweet
i'm sorry
that every time i say "i love you"
it taste sour in my mouth
i'm sorry
that i'm too damaged to believe you
i'm sorry
that i offend you every time you say
you can't live without me
i'm sorry
that the world hasn't been so kind to me
and i find it strange when you are
i'm sorry
that i was never taught how to love correctly
i'm sorry
that i get so scared and lay in bed thinking
of how i can't be what you need
i'm sorry
i was always terrible at new beginnings
and letting go

i'm still learning

i want to teach my daughter
that she is resilient
that she comes from a woman
who had to pick up her own pieces
and sew herself again once more
with shaky hands and glazed eyes
i want to teach my daughter
that she is whole
that she will always be whole
although the pieces aren't together anymore
they're all still there
i want to teach my daughter
that she is love
that she is light
and no man will ever diminish her glow

she'll be stronger than me

i'm a bit older now
and i've realized a lot
i always thought you left
because you didn't love me
which wasn't the case at all
you left because you couldn't
bare the thought of losing me
i was everything you wanted
and you knew it

you didn't deserve me.

there is no right or wrong way to healing
if you must watch those old videos
where he sang that dumb song in his bedroom
then do it
if you must scroll through all your old text messages
and reminisce on the good old times
then do it
if you must stare at that picture of him
the one where his hair is all messed up
and his eyes are squinted from the flash
then do it
and if you must burn all of your pictures
and delete all of the texts
if you must give him back his sweatshirt
that you've been sleeping in ever since he left
then do it.

you heal on your own time.

i'm terrified of love
not because it doesn't last forever
but because sometimes it does

i know i am a good person
but i believe the universe doesn't
from all of the unfortunate things
that has happened to me
i lay in bed with a tender soul
and wonder why i hurt so easily
and wonder what i did
in a past life
to get all of this karma

sometimes we'll never get the answers
like why couldn't you have loved me
the way you are loving her?
sometimes it's nothing personal
like the time i broke that boy's heart
"a fire has been set in my soul" i said
"and only one person can put it out"
it wasn't that i didn't love him
it was that, my love for him
wasn't as strong as mine for the other boy
in the end i got my heart broken
and i was always sat there wondering
why people never wanted to love
the ones who deserved it.

to the one who was in love with me, i'm sorry.

i underestimate how powerful i actually am
i can move mountains and calm oceans
i could laugh and sing and dance and cry
i can love and learn and break and die
i'm fragile and strong at the same time

please don't hate who hurt you

please don't hate who hurt you. understand it wasn't easy for them either. understand that their heart hurt too. they didn't mean to hurt you. life isn't so easy sometimes. sometimes love isn't all that you need. i know it feels like they didn't care, but trust me, they did. they cared. who couldn't live with the guilt of breaking another person?

i remember when you first broke my heart. i called you an asshole and said i wished i hadn't fallen in love with you in the first place. i didn't realize how many sleepless nights you had, trying to convince yourself to stay. i went through the same thing. i broke another person too. and i feel as if i broke myself furthermore.

so please do not hate who hurt you.

i guarantee you, it hurt them more.

i was face to face
with the boy who broke my heart
and i didn't want to collapse anymore

i never belonged to you

i always used to believe my heart was yours. and my being was in sync with your breath. our time apart has made me realize something.

i never belonged to you. my heart was never really mine, so who am i to give it up?

i belong to lovers who have been broken. i belong to all the people who had their chance and missed it. i belong to the loving people in coffee shops, who put a little too much honey in their tea. i belong to the oceans that don't sleep. i belong to the books that broke your heart, mended it, then smashed it again. i belong to the restless nights. i belong to the lost souls who are up at 3am replaying memories in their head. i belong to subway stations and the passenger's side of a car that was going a little too fast on the highway. i belong to every tree that has died and had been reborn.

so no.

i never belonged to you.

i belonged to the world. and it'd be foolish of me to give myself away, to the boy, who can't make up his mind.

it's the sad truth
that some people
are meant to love each other
but aren't meant to be together

acceptance

i've come to learn
promises are meant to break
and sadly, hearts take the stake
but i've also come to know
that there's love in our veins
and hope in our soul

choose happiness.

my inner peace is getting stronger
my poems have become longer
my eyes aren't crying like before
i'm slowly closing that door

standing at the edge with an open heart
and open eyes and beautiful art
i'll become something great
it's etched in the sky

there were nights i yelled at the stars
"i defy you, you make life hard"
had it been easier if i just moved on
instead standing at that closed door for so long?

be gentle.
be kind.
love.

you are alive

when i'm sad nothing else matters. my entire body shuts down, and everything that i was excited about is no longer important. i am alive.
i am alive in the moments where my chest gets heavy from the hurt. i am alive from the way my body shakes uncontrollably when i think of pain. i am alive in every step i take and every thing i say. i am alive when i sit in the trunk of my friend's car, under the stars, and talk about everything that breaks me. i am alive in the way i look for the good in people. i am alive in every person i loved. a piece of me is embedded into them because i loved ferociously. i am alive in the moments i feel i am not.
i am alive in the way i escape the world's madness by staring at the stars, thinking, "wow, the next time i look up, my entire life will be so different." and perhaps the stars are staring back down at me, thinking, "if i were there with her, if i got the chance to know her, i would've loved her."
i am alive.
especially in the moments i feel i am not.

let art be your escape.

i know your heart hurts. and i know your chest feels heavy
with each breath you take. i know you were always afraid
of love because it never did you any good in the end. i know
you wish upon stars, begging them to realign. i know your
mind is brought upon a person while reading this. i know you
think of their smile and the curl of their fingertips. and i know
whenever you close your eyes they're all you see. you don't
want them to be on your mind all the time, i know you don't.
but there's something there. it's almost as if your heart and
their heart have connecting strings that lead all the way back
to the sun. i know, love hurts more than anything. i know that
you've cried so many tears and prayed so many times, wishing,
wishing, wishing. i know you wanted so badly for them to be
the one because if they weren't then what would you do?
i know some days are easier than others.
i know your eyes are glossed over from the memories.
i know it won't be easy, but i also know, you'll get through this.

take it one day at a time.

you say
"i need you"

you need me, to love you
and care for you, to be there
when your world is falling apart
and every time karma
takes a jab at your soul

i reply
"i need me"

i need me, to pick myself up
and to love my flaws
the way i loved yours
and understand my worth
because i haven't
done anything for myself
but i gave you the world

i regret letting you have so much power over me.

love isn't the culprit
love wasn't the one who broke your heart
love wasn't responsible for the downfall
love was there at the edge of your bed when he left
next to the pile of laundry you refuse to fold
love was there on those sleepless nights
begging you to get some rest
please don't blame love
for the universe's plans
she wanted things to end differently
but just like you, it was out of love's hands.

he loved her for everything she was and she loved him for everything he could have been.

do not become mesmerized by the color of his eyes
you don't know the storm brewing behind them

i am the human form of exhaustion
oh so, bittersweet
i am the prime example of fear
glass beneath my feet

i am all the things
you could've said
i am the messy thoughts
that lie within your head

so when i ask you to strip yourself
and become who you're supposed to be
it's not to make fun of you
in such vulnerability

i'm simply asking you
to take your broken heart
and gracefully
turn it into art

reborn.

learning to love again

i swore he felt like home, the home i've always dreamt of and the one i longed for dearly.
after that night my entire world seemed to flip in the most amazing way. i knew i wanted to be with him, entirely. but a part of me always thought he belonged to someone else who could be everything he's always wanted.
every time i saw him i felt as if my head belonged on his chest, listening to his heart beat. listening to the sound of his breathing as he drifted off to sleep. but these were just dreams that would never be proven to happen.
and most times reality comes back and hits me. so i ignore my feelings for him; only for him to ignite it once more the minute he smiles at me.
he eases me. my frantic soul and wavering emotions calmed by the sound of his voice.
i swore he felt like home.

he says he loves me
i respond i love him more
he tells me there's no proof
but in my mind he made a home
and my heart he's made it grown

i write his name in the sand
and smile at birds who sing
sketching poems on coffee shop napkins
his lips on my mind and hands on my skin
and my entire body radiates when he smiles

i love him more than writing
and more than early mornings with my dogs
more than a quiet afternoon
more than admiring the moon
and more than the books i escape to

i love him so much
that i've conquered the fear of heartbreak
i love him so much that
i've finally opened my heart back up
and allowed him to fill it with love

so when i say i love him more
i don't mean i love him more than he loves me
i love him more than all of the things i love combined
and i love him more than purple flowers
i love him because he gives me peace of mind.

the sun belongs to the day
the moon belongs to the night
but when the sun begins to fade away
it still shines so bright

i compare him to the sun
and i know i resemble the moon
as if god created us as one
destined for our love to bloom

as if we fell for each other
but belonged to someone else
we were supposed to be with one another
but seemed to miss every chance we got

we waited for so long
missing opportunities by taking other paths
but when the eclipse occurred
there was no doubt in my mind that we would last.

pray that you never frown
and the sound of my name
that you heart doesn't let go
while mine holds on so dearly

i pray the rest of my life
is spent with your smile
and that you never lose
your radiant light

i pray i'll never forget
how you made me feel
when we danced in your room
to the end credits of titanic

i pray that years from now
it's my name that rolls
off your tongue when people
ask what happiness is

i pray that it's you and me
forever and always.

wars between lovers
are the most deadly
you're everything i love
and everything i've fought for
why are we going against each other?

you say you'll stop
and i say i'll try
but sometimes we
don't see eye to eye
we might as well be blind

you have the key
to make me happy
to make all the sadness
melt away, disintegrate
but in war it's here to stay

throw down your weapons
and come to my arms
where you belong
leave the wars to foes
love is all we should know.

we sit on the earth
leaving marks of love
whispering about the stars
and the clouds up above

we stare at the moon
and he tells me stories
of shooting stars he's seen
and wonders what they mean

angels cry when we're sad
and they radiate when we laugh
they sing along when we dance
and reassure we didn't meet by chance

i remember the cracks in my heart
others only put bandaids on
but he's mended my being
by kissing my soul and loving my art
thank you for loving me.

it's not fair to you
my emotions are reckless
and everything you do i end up breathless
like you're a savior but you're only a man
i swear when you touch my hand
we're radiant
like stars we watch at night
when you walk me home in the cold
it's not your fault
i know i'm always sad
and you hate it when i shut you out
everyone has left
but for some reason you stay
no matter what i say, how awful i can be
please don't go
be patient, you see
i'm trying to understand
what it's like to be alive
and i try to understand why
you still love me after all this time

through all the stupid fights
and those sleepless nights
i know sometimes i'm not there for you
it hurts me to know i cause you pain
one day it won't be this way
when i get better
and decide to stop being so sad
we'll be okay
no matter what happens
you'll always feel like home
that shields me from the cold
i love you, i promise i do
stay so i can prove it to you.

i've been struggling to write words
the words that will take away the hurt
but since you've come along all i feel is joy
the emotions that have been written by tolstoy

i love you, within these stanzas you'll see
that each and every flaw is perfect to me
you say that i'm not telling the truth
but when i'm with you, my mind you soothe

kiss me good morning
and stay until sunset
stay forever, please
our undying love, we will never forget

i'll caress your hair
as you're sound asleep
and listen to your heart beat
how grateful i am that it beats for me

i love you forever, forever and a day
the words i struggle to write are easier to say
when i see your face and your radiant smile
i am reborn, that's how i know our love is worthwhile.

i read and read these book pages
the highlighted words
remind me of you, and your heart
it's like i knew you
before i knew you
no wonder why you're my home

love me gentle
keep me safe
love me tender
and sweet

kiss my forehead
and laugh with me
love my flaws
and be there through everything

all of these things
you do extraordinary well
each and every day
more in love i fell

from your smile
to your eyes
to your spiraled hair
to your fears

i love every bit of you
every broken piece
i must stick back together
with glue

i love you tender
i love you passionately
our lives contain greatness
we are meant to be.

it's 3 am
and i miss your touch
i miss your smile
i miss your voice

your presence heals me
like you're medicine
your heart is pure
and your love saves me

so unhappy i was before
living day by day sad
sleepless nights, i would cry
but you came and gave me hope

you're a healer
you're more powerful than you think
you have so much good in you
a beautiful wonderful being

stay with me
and brighten the future
with your mind and kind words
with your empathy and loving soul

i search my over read books
for things i feel
in times of sadness
when you're not here

how is it that
fictional characters understand
the love i have for you perfectly
are you even real?

these lines tear me apart
dissecting my insecurities
and making me realize
how much it would hurt if you leave

but you're not leaving
because my head tells me you're not
is this what love feels like
pure and safe certainty?

even in our darkest moments
when you don't want to speak to me
i know we will be okay the next day
because love will always find a way.

you're my morning cup of coffee
that i tell my bizarre dreams to
the one that i nuzzle my chest in
when my head breaks my heart again
my heart is still learning to be okay
thank you for your patience.

i'm grieving the loss of you
before i've even lost you
i need to stop overthinking

today the thunder woke you up and you said you felt sad
i wanted to be your safe haven... the one you can run to
when the storm seems too unbearable and you can't
understand why. i'll be there, your guide. your helping hand.
your peace of mind. allow me to love you, it breaks my heart
when you're distant. it tears me apart. i know i wasn't so kind
to you and everything felt so hopeless.
but we've made it through so much of the storm stronger we
will become, we will be reborn. there's many more stanzas i
could create but i'll end it with these words.
you are radiant. my love, being with you is the one thing i've
done right

i take a look at myself
when you lay me down
and kiss my soul
i am electric

headlights blur together
through the tears
you sit in the passenger seat
and tell me all your fears

in these times we're united
but the next day we're not
communication between us seizes
like we're worlds apart

when you're in that other world
think of those headlights
and replace the stars with those memories
even worlds apart i pray you choose me

have your way with words that sting
and i'll just stay while the trees sing
soothing songs, that ease my soul
make me feel like i am whole
build a home in the forest
say you love me and we'll flourish

i'll run back each time i cry
hunched over, wondering why
leave my heart unbroken, please
leave my words engraved in trees
remember my love and smile ear to ear
love is never wasted that's why i'm still here

this is where we get tangled up
in bed sheets and kisses
with your hand on my back
i freeze at your touch

our hearts are connected
by strings, the cosmos arranged
our strings are not just knotted
they are always in each other's way

so i take a step back
and you're pulled toward me
colliding our lips almost involuntarily
this is where we get tangled up

i stare into the water's reflection
my tears had left a puddle
leave me alone
to feel everything on my own

i know you want the best for me
the angels do too
but i can't let you see me break
because you'll break too

so stay far away
as i sort out my mess
this ocean i call my emotions
and you're the shipwreck

you bought me coffee on our first date
a hazelnut beginning of love in the heat wave
we walk the streets hand in hand
you ask how i have been and i say great
i'm so great
for months i watched you afar
admiring everything you are
and i am glad to call you mine

you see the parts of me
i didn't even know could be seen
and you love me through everything
through every pointless fight
and all those painful sleepless nights
for months i watched you from afar
admiring everything you are
and i am glad to call you mine

i don't want to lose you
but i can't lose myself either
of all the losses in my lifetime
i know yours would break me
i dream of days where we're whole
happily reinventing ourselves
becoming one with each other
like the sun and moon on an eclipse
watering each other piece by piece
until we're regrown and strong

you were always the sun

if tomorrow we fade to gray
you can sit there and say
i followed you every step of the way
and if this lifetime isn't the best
i'll wait until i meet you in the next

the universe will make sure all problems step aside for the
things that are meant to be

today is a new day
let the sunlight in
breathe
sit with yourself
and learn who you are
learn what you want to achieve
and put your mind to it
today is a good day
to let the light in
and be happy

to my person,
you have always been the sun. you have watered my dead
roots and patched my broken petals. you have taught me how
to enjoy life no matter the circumstances. you have shown me
true love, the love that builds me up.
you have made me blossom.
you have made me more attentive to life and my mental health.
you will never know just how much i needed you when i wrote
those first two passages. looking back now, you were always
there. i wish i admitted it to myself sooner.
thank you for showing me the world in a much more beautiful
light, and pushing me to discover myself and become who i was
always afraid to be.
my world wouldn't be the same if you hadn't crashed into it.
but i'm so glad you did.

yours truly, chanteli.

CPSIA information can be obtained
at www.ICGtesting.com
Printed in the USA
BVHW030929080421
604475BV00007B/994

9 781637 283455